EATING
ETHICALLY

by Rebecca Felix

Content Consultant
Alex Kojo Anderson, PhD
Associate Professor of Nutrition
University of Georgia

Core Library

An Imprint of Abdo Publishing
abdopublishing.com

abdopublishing.com

Published by Abdo Publishing, a division of ABDO, PO Box 398166,
Minneapolis, Minnesota 55439. Copyright © 2016 by Abdo Consulting
Group, Inc. International copyrights reserved in all countries. No part of
this book may be reproduced in any form without written permission from
the publisher. Core Library™ is a trademark and logo of Abdo Publishing.

Printed in the United States of America, North Mankato, Minnesota
042015
092015

Cover Photo: Greg Baker/AP Images
Interior Photos: Greg Baker/AP Images, 1; Xi Xin Xing/iStockphoto, 4;
Paul Sakuma/AP Images, 7; Dmitry Kalinovsky/Shutterstock Images, 12,
45; iStockphoto, 15; North Wind Picture Archives, 17; Charlie Riedel/
AP Images, 19; Pavel L./Shutterstock Images, 22; Rebecca Blackwell/AP
Images, 32; Toby Talbot/AP Images, 35; Nati Harnik/AP Images, 37

Editor: Mirella Miller
Series Designer: Becky Daum

Library of Congress Control Number: 2015931587

Cataloging-in-Publication Data
Felix, Rebecca.
 Eating ethically / Rebecca Felix.
   p. cm. -- (Food matters)
Includes bibliographical references and index.
ISBN 978-1-62403-861-7
1. Food--Moral and ethical aspects--Juvenile literature. 2. Food--
Environmental aspects--Juvenile literature. 3. Food--Social aspects--
Juvenile literature.   I. Title.
178--dc23
                                                    2015931587

CONTENTS

CHAPTER ONE

WHAT IS EATING ETHICALLY?

t is time for your favorite part of the school day: lunch! You join the school lunch line. Today's menu includes chicken strips. You fill your tray and rush to your table, where your friends are eating bagged lunches. One friend is eating a turkey sandwich. Another has a brownie for dessert. When lunch ends, everyone throws their leftovers away. Your friend tosses half a sandwich. You dump two chicken strips.

You probably do not think too much about where your food comes from as you go through the school lunch line.

You took more than you could eat, and you do not want to get too full. Your dad is making his famous burgers at home tonight!

It was a typical lunch. You laughed with your friends and ate. But did you think about what you ate? You probably picked items you thought tasted good. Or maybe you chose foods you knew were good for you. But did you think about where your foods came from? Where did the chicken strips come from before the school kitchen? Was the chocolate in your friend's brownie shipped from overseas? You know throwing foods away is wasteful. But did you know all your food choices affect other people, as well as animals and the environment?

Bigger, Faster, Cheaper

Food production involves every part of the economy. It takes energy, transportation, and agriculture to produce foods. Production has become more industrialized over the past century. Today's food industry is focused on producing foods quickly and

It is likely any chicken you cook at home comes from a factory farm.

cheaply. But many parts of food production have become harmful to consumers.

Animal, Environmental, and Human Rights Abuse

More than 99 percent of US chickens are raised on factory farms. Most chickens raised on factory farms never see the sun or grass. They often live in a huge shed packed so tightly with thousands of other chickens that they cannot spread their wings. Chickens on factory farms may wade in piles of waste that is cleaned from the shed only once a year. This waste pollutes groundwater and nearby rivers when it is flushed out of the shed.

Waste from cows raised to become hamburger also pollutes nearby land and water. The cows are crowded in small pens and denied proper care. Such farming methods have widespread effects.

Food production affects the environment in other ways too. Often foods grown in North America are shipped overseas, creating air

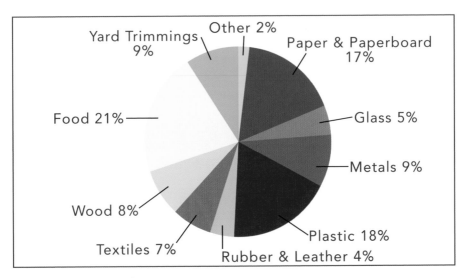

Yard Trimmings 9%

Other 2%

Paper & Paperboard 17%

Food 21%

Glass 5%

Metals 9%

Wood 8%

Plastic 18%

Textiles 7%

Rubber & Leather 4%

Throwing Food Away

Producing an abundance of food and throwing it away is unethical. Throwing food away is also a waste of the resources used to grow or raise, process, package, and transport those foods. Above is a graph of the types of garbage created in the United States in 2010. Are you surprised to see food makes up the largest percentage? Knowing this information, how can you change what you throw away in your daily life?

pollution and using up resources and energy. Many imported foods come from large corporations. This can impact people negatively because large corporations may force smaller farmers to sell their crops for low prices. The corporations then raise prices so they can make more money, which they often do not share with their workers. Some large food corporations even use slaves to grow foods.

Even if all foods came from farmers who did not abuse animals, the environment, or workers, your actions still could have a negative effect on the world. Wasting foods is a disservice to hungry or starving people. Enough foods are produced each year to feed the world. But billions of tons of perfectly good foods are thrown away. Americans throw away approximately half their food every year!

Becoming Aware

How can unfair food practices take place without people demanding they stop? Many people have no idea these practices take place. The food industry is in the business of selling foods for profit. Corporations spend large amounts of money to advertise foods in a positive way. They do not provide the public information about unethical practices. If people knew about animal, environment, or human abuse, they might be less likely to buy certain food products.

Most people try to live ethically. This means they try not to steal, cheat, cause damage, or hurt others. Living ethically involves being a good, kind, and fair person. Eating ethically involves buying and eating foods produced without abuse to animals, the environment, or humans. The first step in learning to eat ethically is understanding how your foods make it to your fork.

CHAPTER TWO

EATING FOR ANIMAL RIGHTS

A cow stands on concrete inside a shed. It has never been outdoors. Its udder is so swollen the cow could almost trip over it, if it had room to move around. The cow stands in its own waste until its bones become weak and snap.

Animals that cannot walk are called "downers" on industrial farms. These animals are exhausted from abuse. Many spend their lives lying on a cement

At some farms, the pens that pigs live in are so small the animals cannot move.

floor. They are covered in waste or trampled by other animals. Their deaths are often just as inhumane.

Industrial Animal Abuse

Many pigs raised on industrial farms spend their lives in metal pens. Some pigs gnaw and push against the bars until their snouts bleed. There have been cases of these animals being fed actual garbage, including crushed glass and used syringes. Activists Miyun Park and Moby, who is also a singer, wrote a book called *Gristle*, which deals with the problems of factory farms. In the book, Park and Moby say that when we eat animals, we eat what they eat. They talk about how some factory-farmed animals are fed animal waste, as well as the blood, fat, and bone waste left over from other animals' slaughter.

Chickens bred to lay eggs live in small cages with several chickens squeezed together. When the chickens stop laying eggs, their bodies are of no use. The farmers must get rid of them.

Many chickens at poultry farms have the ends of their beaks removed so they do not peck each other.

Many animal abuse discoveries have been made by undercover animal rights organizations. Several meat-processing plants were shut down after the Humane Society showed evidence of terrible conditions inside the plants. Some workers were even arrested. But many states have made it illegal to work undercover in the agriculture industry. That means abuse will stay behind closed doors, along with the animals. As of 2014, more than 99 percent of US farm animals were raised on factory farms. How did these industrial operations become the norm?

Ethically Raised Meat

Although the majority of animals are raised on factory farms, it is possible to buy and eat ethically raised meat. Eating meat is part of a healthy diet. Meats have more nutrients than any plants. With an adult's help, research ethical meat companies online. Look for these brands at your local grocery store or ask the grocery store to begin stocking more ethical options.

Many organic farms take good care of their animals. Organic livestock farms raise small numbers of animals. This allows the farmer to provide the necessary care for each

An Industrial Chicken Shed

Most chickens sold in supermarkets are raised in crowded indoor sheds of 30,000 or more birds. Inside these sheds, chickens cover the floor, smashed against each other. They stand on top of piles of waste. The waste gives off so much ammonia the birds' eyes water. They develop blisters from the chemical. Some of the birds die of starvation. They are unable to get through the sea of birds to reach their food source.

The Chicago stockyard was the model for many large stockyards built across the Midwest in the 1900s.

animal. These farmers take time to make sure their animals are fed the correct foods, have space to move around, and have clean living spaces.

History of Intensive Farming

In the late 1800s, the transcontinental railroad was completed, linking the United States from coast to coast. This allowed cattle to be transported across the country. Chicago was home to a huge stockyard. By 1900, stockyard workers had slaughtered 400 million animals. Companies shipped the meat across the country. To keep up with new demand, the workers used conveyor belts and machines to move and process the animals.

When World War II (1939–1945) ended, the government wanted to use war-production factories for the meatpacking industry. Livestock and poultry were moved inside these factories. The animals' environments were controlled so they would grow larger and produce more meat. Farmers used farmland to grow massive amounts of one kind of crop, which was more efficient. The yields of both livestock and crops rose greatly.

YOUR LIFE
What Would You Do?

Not all industrial farms treat their animals as terribly as those mentioned in Chapter Two. But undercover investigations have proven several do. Would you be able to witness the scenes described in this chapter? What would you say or do? In what ways could farms improve treatment of their animals?

Some animals in large farms are treated poorly before they are killed to be made into food.

Improved production made government and agricultural companies believe bigger was better. Traditional farmers struggled to match their superfast production and cheap prices. But to make a profit, industrial farmers cut corners. Many chose not to spend money on providing proper care for the animals. Industrial farms grew more and more crowded.

In 1950 there was an average of 19 pigs per farm. By 2005 there were several thousand pigs on some farms. Poultry farms were even more crowded. In 1950 there were 50,000 poultry farms and 630 million chickens in the country. By 2005 there were 30,000 farms and 8.7 billion chickens. As the number of animals per farm increases, their quality of life decreases. And few laws are in place to stop the abuse.

Fighting for Rights

The Animal Welfare Act passed in 1966 covers farm animals' rights to food, fresh air, and exercise, but only during transport. And this law does not apply to birds. Neither does the federal Humane Methods of Slaughter Act. It says animals are to be made senseless before being killed. Many industrial farms have rules in place to do this. But undercover investigations have found many do not actually follow the rules.

The Humane Society released a shocking undercover report in 2008. It revealed abuse and violence witnessed in a cattle slaughterhouse through gruesome descriptions:

> *A shocking undercover investigation by The Humane Society of the United States reveals widespread mistreatment of 'downed' dairy cows—those who are too sick or injured to walk—at a Southern California slaughter plant. . . .*
>
> *Cruelties that Defy Belief*
>
> *In the video, workers are seen kicking cows, ramming them with the blades of a forklift, jabbing them in the eyes, applying painful electrical shocks and even torturing them with a hose and water in attempts to force sick or injured animals to walk to slaughter.*

Source: "Rampant Animal Cruelty at California Slaughter Plant." The Humane Society of the United States. *The Humane Society of the United States, January 30, 2008. Web. Accessed January 22, 2015.*

Changing Minds

Take a position on the treatment of downed animals at the California slaughterhouse. Imagine your best friend has the opposite opinion. Write a letter trying to change your friend's mind. Make sure you explain your opinion. Include facts and details that support your case.

EATING FOR THE ENVIRONMENT

n traditional farming, farmers balance the amount of waste their livestock creates with the area of land they have. They make sure not to overload soil with waste it cannot absorb. On industrial farms, animal waste piles up indoors. It is cleaned out every so often. Then it is released into the environment, where it pollutes air, land, and water.

Many industrial farms may not dispose of their animals' waste in proper ways.

Waste and Gases

Farm animals in the United States produce three times the waste humans make each year. Waste is flushed from sheds into large holding pools. It often leaks into nearby soil and water systems. Groundwater can become contaminated and unsafe for humans to drink. The waste also leaks into rivers and bays. Its nutrients cause algae to grow. The algae wipe out other forms of life. The waste that breaks down in the air gives off polluting gases.

Traditional farming uses animal manure and other natural processes to fertilize soil for crops. But people developed ways to spray chemical fertilizers in the 1900s. For the past 100 years, large farms have sprayed fertilizer on fields using machinery. This is a much easier and faster process than spreading manure. The tradeoff is that making fertilizer gives off greenhouse gases. An excess of greenhouse gases, natural or man-made, trap heat in Earth's atmosphere, which creates global warming. Global warming can cause long-term climate change and unusual weather patterns. It also can lead to the extinction of species that cannot survive the changing temperatures. Producing the fertilizer used for crops that feed livestock gives off as much greenhouse gas each year as 7 million cars!

Once the crops are grown, they are transported to animal feeding operations. It takes energy to heat and cool indoor sheds on these industrial feedlots. Machines used to slaughter the animals also use energy. In 2006 the United Nations reported that raising livestock was responsible for 18 percent

Nature's Greenhouse Gas

Cows, sheep, and goats are ruminants. This means they have stomachs with different compartments. They eat plant material they cannot digest. The plant material becomes partially digested in one of the stomach compartments. Then the animals regurgitate the plant material. Methane from inside the animals' stomachs is released during regurgitation. The animals chew on the plant material some more, until it becomes cud. Eventually the animals swallow the cud.

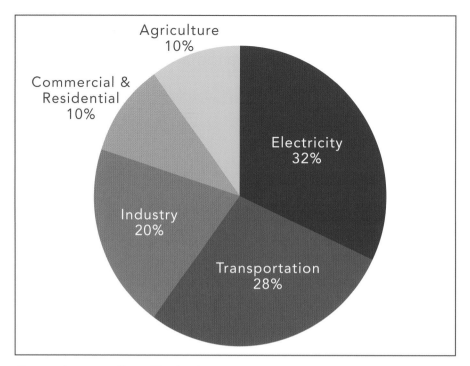

Greenhouse Gas Emissions

The US Environmental Protection Agency reported each economic sector's percentage of greenhouse gas emissions in 2012. Agriculture is directly responsible for 10 percent, but which other categories are used by the food industry?

of the world's greenhouse gas emissions. This was more than the world's entire transportation system.

Livestock naturally give off the greenhouse gas methane. This is a part of their digestive process. It has always occurred on farms. But because industrial farms have many more animals than traditional ones, a much greater amount of gas is being given off.

Transportation and Garbage

The average distance foods are hauled in developed nations has become four times longer since 1961. Foods are trucked around the country. They are flown and shipped across the planet. This is so people can eat foods from other cultures or have foods that are not in season where they live.

Many people believe it is more ethical to eat foods grown locally. But this is not always the greener or more environmentally friendly choice. Peter Singer and Jim Mason are the authors of *The Ethics of What We Eat.* In their book, they follow several families as they shop for foods. One woman buys tomatoes directly from a local farmer. She thinks she is buying a green product, but the farmer used an oil furnace to keep his plants warm so his tomatoes would grow all year. The tomatoes in the woman's local grocery store were shipped across the country, but their transport gave off fewer greenhouse gases than the local farmer's oil use. In this case, the local

Air Pollution

People who live near industrial farms often breathe in the gases released as animal waste breaks down. People living near these farms have reported sore throats, diarrhea, wheezing, and more. If you lived near an industrial farm, what would you do? Would you be more concerned about its environmental issues? Would you ask the farmers to make changes? Would you reach out to your local government for help?

choice was worse for the environment.

Many foods people eat today are packaged. This packaging ends up in landfills. And creating and disposing of it uses a great deal of resources and energy.

Reducing Food Waste

Some people choose to eat meat only some nights of the week. On the nights they do not include meat in their meals, they cook vegetarian dishes. They believe that by cutting meat out of their diets a few times per week, they are helping reduce the demand for factory farm-raised animals. Ethical brands from the local grocery store or farmer's market are smart options.

People can help cut back on food waste by taking smaller portions at meals. If you cannot finish all of the food at a restaurant, take home the leftovers. When saving leftovers at home, use plastic or glass containers. You can also eliminate waste by recycling or starting a compost pile. When you're at the grocery store, look for foods that have little packaging. This can prevent unnecessary waste.

Using Resources

Raising livestock uses a lot of energy. It takes more than 2,400 gallons (9,085 L) of water and 13 pounds (6 kg) of grain feed to produce 1 pound (0.5 kg) of meat. Raising livestock takes up to 30 percent of the world's land mass. The world's forests are being bulldozed to make room for animals to graze and to grow crops to feed them.

Earth's waters are affected by industrial farming practices. Every year, people eat 100 million tons

(91 million metric tons) of seafood. Huge fishing boat nets capture tons of fish, as well as other animals. The bycatch, or unwanted animals, are thrown overboard. They are already dead or dying. Each year this adds up to 27 million tons (25 million metric tons) of trashed marine life.

Overfishing has caused some marine species to become threatened. Overfishing is a danger to the environment, as well as to people's ways of life.

FURTHER EVIDENCE

Chapter Three has a great deal of information about how food production damages and pollutes the environment. This chapter talks about livestock being a main contributor. Check out the website at the link below. Can you find information on the site that supports the author's point? Write a few sentences using information from the website as evidence to support the main point of this chapter.

Sustainable Table
mycorelibrary.com/eating-ethically

Overfishing depletes the ocean of life, often threatening to completely wipe out entire marine species. The Save Our Seas Foundation, an organization dedicated to marine preservation, details this threat on their website:

> The statistics are grim: 3/4 of the world's fish stocks are being harvested faster than they can reproduce. Eighty percent are already fully exploited or in decline. Ninety percent of all large predatory fish—including tuna, sharks, swordfish, cod and halibut—are gone. Scientists predict that if current trends continue, world food fisheries could collapse entirely by 2050.
>
> The most prized species are already disappearing. The 1990s saw the widely-publicised collapse of several major cod fisheries, which have failed to recover even after fishing was stopped.

Source: "Threat 1: Overfishing." Save Our Seas Foundation. *Save Our Seas Foundation, 2014. Web. Accessed January 22, 2015.*

What's the Big Idea?

Take a close look at this text from the Save Our Seas Foundation website. What is the author's main point about the future of marine life? Pick out two details the author uses to make this point. If you had to write the purpose of this text in one sentence, what would it say?

EATING FOR HUMAN RIGHTS

Do you like chocolate? Many people do. Chocolate is in US supermarkets, stores, movie theaters, and more. It is everywhere! Nearly half of the cocoa the world uses to make chocolate is sourced from Africa's Ivory Coast.

The Ivory Coast has many documented cases of child trafficking. This involves kidnapping children and treating them as possessions. The children are sold

Investigations of some African farms have found not all crops are produced in an ethical way.

to farmers and put to work as slaves. They never see their families and are not allowed to go to school. They are forced to do difficult and dangerous work.

There are other cases of child and adult slave labor around the world. Foods produced by slave labor include rice, bananas, beef, and coffee. Slaves in the Thai fishing industry are forced to work long hours, are beaten, and are even killed. You can find the shrimp caught by these slaves in grocery stores worldwide. Much of the world's bananas are grown on plantations. Workers live on these farms run by large, nonlocal corporations. Some workers are physically abused. They are paid hardly enough to survive. When the company makes a profit, the workers do not see an increase in pay. To avoid these abuses, a system of fair world trade has been established.

Fair Trade

Fair trade is a system of buying goods from farmers and companies that provide workers with fair wages and treatment. Fair-trade products are priced slightly

A wide variety of fair-trade products are available for purchase, including coffee.

higher than other foods. The extra funds are used for projects in the communities that grow the foods. The communities decide how to best spend the money. Some establish healthcare, educational resources, or shelter. Others create programs to empower women workers. Special "Fair Trade" labels are used to mark overseas products from companies that treat workers fairly. But many workers in the United States are treated unfairly without a prevention program in place.

Fair-Trade Payoffs

More people are becoming aware of human rights issues in food importing. Fair-trade programs have grown in recent decades. As of 2012, there were 1,139 organizations and 70 countries involved in fair trade.

Factory Farms

People who work on industrial farms use dangerous machinery. They work with animals that may be diseased. They also work around large amounts of animal waste that gives off dangerous gases. Studies

Slaughterhouse jobs can be dangerous.

have found many industrial farm workers have respiratory problems.

Slaughtering animals is dangerous to workers' health. Some slaughterhouse workers have scars and even amputations. Many slaughterhouse workers are paid very poorly. Some are not skilled and have a hard time finding other jobs. However, current industrial farms also have opportunities in food packaging, transportation, and storage.

Convenience, Efficiency, and Cost

Some people argue that raising animals indoors is more humane. It allows farmers to keep the animals out of extreme cold and heat. They say it is easier to monitor the animals. But other industrial farm workers say monitoring is impossible. Workers do not have the time to check on thousands of animals each day.

Raising animals in massive numbers relates to industrial farming's main argument. A growing population of people demands a larger food supply. Many people believe industrial farming methods are the only way to meet this demand. Supporters of industrial agriculture say its practices increase food security, providing more food for people in need. A University of Michigan study says differently. Researchers found average organic farms in developed countries produced about the same amount of foods as those of industrial farms. In developing countries, organic farms produced more foods than industrial farms.

Ethical alternatives can also be more expensive. Providing animals with proper nutrition, space, and care costs farms more money. So fair-trade products are priced higher than foods that are not fair trade. But many people believe the true cost of food produced unethically is hidden. It is paid in other ways, by animals, the environment, and people. Is it possible to find ethically produced foods easily? Is it affordable? And will changing the way you eat have an impact on food production? Many experts, researchers, and traditional farmers think so.

YOUR LIFE
Making Changes?

Has reading about ethics in food production inspired you to change the way you eat or to ask questions about the foods you eat? What can you do to eat more ethically? For example, you may decide to buy only fair-trade foods. If you are shopping at a supermarket, how will you find fair-trade foods?

Ethical Eating Tips and Tools

Some people become vegan as they attempt to eat ethically. Others become vegetarian. Some eat vegan or vegetarian meals a couple times a week. If enough people did this, less livestock would need to be raised, using fewer resources and creating less pollution. This would free up many crops that are currently used to feed livestock.

Doing research and reading labels is another way to eat ethically. Shoppers can look for the Fair Trade certification label on imported foods. They can find lists of fair-trade products online. Many activists say the best way to ensure ethical eating is to ask questions about foods before buying and consuming them. They say people can ask for ethical foods. At restaurants people can ask where the meat in the hamburgers comes from or if the chocolate in the desserts is fair trade. People can ask supermarket managers to point out ethical brands. Students can ask their principals if the foods their schools provide created the least greenhouse gas emissions possible. Many people likely will not have answers to these questions. But activists believe asking for answers will show a demand for ethical practices and products, leading to more people eating ethically.

EXPLORE ONLINE

Chapter Four features arguments defending industrial farming and current food-production practices. The website below lists possible benefits to these farming methods. How is the information on this website different from the information in this chapter? What information is the same? How do the two sources present information differently? What can you learn from this website?

Food and Agriculture Organization
mycorelibrary.com/eating-ethically

- Most agricultural products are produced on industrial farms. Huge fields of one type of crop are planted on these farms. Chemical fertilizer is used to help plants grow bigger. Crops are transported to livestock industrial farms, where they are fed to animals.

- Extreme crowding and animal abuse are common. Animals live in their own waste, die from stress, and are handled poorly.

- Industrial livestock farms produce large amounts of waste. This waste pollutes the air, land, and waterways. The waste breaks down and releases greenhouse gases that contribute to global warming.

- Some large farms that grow foods for export overseas use child and slave labor. Others do not treat workers fairly. Workers are paid very low wages, and the companies they work for profit from selling the foods overseas.

IN THE KITCHEN

Vegan and Fair-Trade Cookies

3 ripe, Fair Trade–Certified bananas

1 teaspoon Fair Trade–Certified vanilla extract

1/4 cup unsweetened applesauce

1/4 cup Fair Trade–Certified agave nectar

1/2 cup canola oil

1 tablespoon coconut milk

1 cup oat flour

1 teaspoon baking soda

1 teaspoon Fair Trade–Certified cinnamon

1 cup rolled oats

1 cup shredded coconut

Preheat the oven to 350 degrees Fahrenheit (177°C). Put the bananas, vanilla, applesauce, agave nectar, oil, and coconut milk in a large bowl. Have an adult help you blend it. Add the flour, baking soda, and cinnamon. Mix it up. Pour the oats and coconut in, and then use your hands to mix the dough together. Roll into 1-inch (2.5-cm) balls on a cookie sheet and bake for 18 to 20 minutes.

STOP AND THINK

Surprise Me

All chapters in this book discuss hidden aspects of food production. Many of these facts can be surprising or even shocking to people. After reading this book, what two or three facts about current food-production processes did you find most surprising? Write a few sentences about each fact. Then explain why you find them surprising.

Another View

This book has information about how some industrial farm practices can be unethical. However, as you know, every source is different. Ask an adult, such as a librarian, to help you find another source about industrial farming. Research and then write a short essay comparing and contrasting the new source's point of view with that of this book's author. What is each author's point of view? How are their views similar or different, and why?

You Are There

This book examines many cases of poor or abusive conditions on industrial farms. Imagine you are a worker on one of these farms. It is time to gather animals for slaughter. What do you see? How do you feel about what is happening?

Say What?

Learning about the food industry can mean learning a great deal of new vocabulary. Find five words in this book that you have never heard before. Use a dictionary to find out what they mean. Then write the meanings in your own words and use each word in a sentence.

GLOSSARY

activists
people who speak out and take action on a controversial issue

contaminated
exposed to something harmful

disservice
actions that harm a person or group of people

empower
to give power to a person or group of people

imported
brought in from another country to be sold

industrialized
built and run similar to a factory

regurgitate
to bring back up food that has been swallowed

stockyard
an enclosed area where farm animals are kept to be slaughtered

syringes
hollow tubes and needles used to insert fluids, usually medicine, into a person or animal

vegan
a person who does not eat foods made from animals, including meat, cheese, eggs, and milk

LEARN MORE

Books

Etingoff, Kim. *Farmed Fish*. Broomall, PA: Mason Crest Publishers, 2014.

Miller, Debra A. *Farming and the Food Supply*. Detroit: Greenhaven Press, 2011.

Singer, Jane E. *Meat*. Broomall, PA: Mason Crest Publishers, 2014.

Websites

To learn more about Food Matters, visit **booklinks.abdopublishing.com**. These links are routinely monitored and updated to provide the most current information available.

Visit **mycorelibrary.com** for free additional tools for teachers and students.

INDEX

ABOUT THE AUTHOR

Rebecca Felix is a writer and editor from Minnesota. She has a bachelor's degree in English from the University of Minnesota-Twin Cities. Rebecca has written dozens of books on many topics for kids of all ages.